PLAY BALL!
Mental Game
Skills for Young
Baseball Players

Balancing Competitive Spirit & Fun on the Road to Success

Johnny Powers

Contents

Welcome To Training!

T wo best friends named Timmy and Bobby laced up their new cleats and tightened their baseball gloves. They were giddy with excitement because this was the summer they were joining the Mighty Cubs, their town's coolest baseball team.

As they stepped onto the sun-drenched field for their first practice, they noticed some players throwing balls farther and running faster than they ever had. Their excitement quickly turned to jitters in their stomachs. They started to worry they weren't good enough to be with the other kids.

Timmy whispered to Bobby, "They're super fast, aren't they?"

Bobby nodded, his eyes wide. "And look at how far they can throw!"

Before they could worry anymore, Coach Andy called them over. He was a tall man with a kind smile. "Alright, Mighty Cubs! It's time to start our drills!"

Timmy and Bobby looked at each other. They gulped, nodded, and ran to join the rest of the team.

First up was the throwing drill. Timmy felt his heart race as he watched the others throw. When it was his turn, his throw wasn't the farthest, but Coach Andy clapped his hands. "Good job, Timmy! That was a solid throw. Keep practicing, and you'll throw even farther."

Next was the running drill. Bobby was worried his legs weren't as fast as the others. When Coach Andy said, "Go!" he ran as fast as he could. He didn't come in first, but Coach Andy gave him a thumbs-up. "Great effort, Bobby! Your speed will improve with time."

By the end of the practice, Timmy and Bobby were out of breath, but they were grinning. They had learned so much from Coach Andy and the other players.

As they gathered their gear to head home, Coach Andy came over. "You guys did a great job today," he said, ruffling their hair. "Remember, everyone starts somewhere. The important thing is to keep trying, keep practicing, and never give up."

That night, Timmy and Bobby weren't worried anymore. They were eager for their next practice. They knew they would get better with time, and they couldn't wait to become the best Mighty Cubs they could be.

From then on, whenever they felt nervous or doubtful, they remembered Coach Andy's words and believed in themselves. After all, they were now part of the Mighty Cubs, and they were ready to give their best.

As the summer days went on, Timmy and Bobby practiced diligently, both during team practices and on their own. They worked on their throws, swings, and sprints, becoming a little better each day. However, they realized that the physical skills were just one part of the game. They also needed something else: mental toughness.

One hot afternoon, while they were practicing throws in Timmy's backyard, Bobby's throw went wild, knocking over a can of soda.

"Oh no," Bobby sighed, looking at the spilled soda. "I messed up."

Timmy picked up the can, wiped it off, and grinned at Bobby. "So what?" he said. "It's not like we're going to quit playing just because you knocked over a soda can."

Bobby smiled back. "You're right. We can clean it up. I'll just try again."

They continued practicing, realizing that it's okay to make mistakes. They just had to pick themselves up and keep going. That was mental toughness.

Another day, while they were at school, they faced a tough math problem. Bobby was ready to give up. "I don't get it," he groaned, dropping his pencil.

But Timmy looked at the problem, then at his friend. "Remember what we learned in baseball?" he asked. "We didn't quit when we made mistakes. We kept trying until we got better. Let's try that here."

They spent the next hour figuring out the problem. It was hard, but they didn't give up. When they finally solved it, they high-fived each other. They realized that mental toughness wasn't just for baseball. It was for all challenges they faced, even math problems.

After that day, their approach to baseball, and life, changed. They started to see each hurdle, whether on the field, at school, or at home, as an opportunity to practice their mental toughness. They understood that this would help them grow stronger and become better at anything they did.

And all through the summer, they held on to this spirit. No matter what happened, they reminded each other, "Remember, we're Mighty Cubs. We never give up!" And just like that, the two friends kept growing, on and off the baseball field, one day at a time.

If you are a young baseball player reading this story, you are probably wondering how you can become a mentally tough athlete. Well, you've come to the right place!

Mental toughness is about always trying your best, working hard, and using mistakes as a way to learn and get better.

The best part? Anybody can learn mental toughness!

This book will help you do your best, not be scared, and feel confident when the game is really close. We'll learn from some of the best baseball players like Babe Ruth and Mike Trout. They all had mental toughness, and this book can help you get it too.

This book isn't just a bunch of fun stories. It's filled with tips and advice to help you become the best player you can be. And don't worry, it's simple and easy to understand, so you won't be bored.

Now, you may be wondering, who is giving all this advice? Well, it's me, and I used to be a really good baseball player. I even set some records and won important games with my team. But most importantly, I know how it feels to be you, and I want to help you be your best.

But remember, learning to be mentally tough isn't always easy. It can be hard, but it's worth it. So, let's get started by busting some myths about mental toughness.

Some people think you have to be born good at sports, but that's not true. Hard work and practice are more important. For example, Derek Jeter, one of the best baseball players ever, said it was his hard work, not just his talent, that made him great.

And remember, you don't have to figure everything out by yourself. Just like Venus and Serena Williams had their dad to help them become tennis stars, you can ask for help too. After all, wouldn't you help your little brother or sister if they needed you?

But it's not just moms, dads, and coaches who can help you. Even the best athletes have a team around them, like trainers and friends who also play sports. They know that they can't do it all by themselves, and they need the help of others.

So, don't try to do everything on your own. Encourage your mom and dad to read books and learn more about kids' sports. It's okay to ask for help as you learn how to play sports.

Some people think that you can't learn mental toughness, but that's not true! Mental toughness is a skill you can get better at. Did you know your mind controls so much of what you do? So, learning to make your mind stronger makes a lot of sense, right?

Even big college and professional sports teams have a person whose job is to help athletes with their mental skills. So, don't wait. Start learning mental toughness now, and you'll be better than your competitors!

This book is for everyone. If you're a young athlete, a coach, or a parent, you can learn from this book. Mental toughness takes time and practice, but if you follow this guide, you'll get better at handling big moments, staying focused and calm, and doing your best when it really counts.

Ready to start?

Chapter 1
Understanding the Power of Mental Toughness

L et's imagine an eight-year-old boy who excitedly tells his parents he dreams of playing for the New York Yankees. Some parents might think this is just kid's talk. But Derek Jeter's parents took him seriously. They told him that if he worked hard and never gave up, he could do anything.

And guess what? Derek Jeter did become a baseball player for the New York Yankees. And not just any player. He was one of the best, with lots of awards and 20 years on the team.

Jeter was known for always being ready to play and staying calm, even when the game was really close. He says his mom and dad taught him how to work hard, take care of himself, and think like a winner.

"You have to work harder than other people if you want to be the best," said Jeter. "Never be satisfied."

Jeter is a great example of an athlete with mental toughness.

In his book, "The Life You Imagine," Jeter shares a 10-step plan for being successful. He used this plan for baseball, but it can help with anything in life. Jeter learned from his experiences and his parents that success isn't just about reaching a goal. It's about making a plan and taking steps every day to reach that goal.

No matter how old you are, Jeter's steps for success can help you reach your dreams.

Here are the 10 steps:

1. Reach for the Stars

Don't be afraid to dream big, even if it seems really, really hard. Your dreams are the engine that powers you to do great things.

2. Overcome Hurdles

There will always be things that stand in your way. When Jeter first started playing professional baseball, he had trouble hitting the ball. It was tough, but he knew he had to keep trying to reach his dream.

3. Learn from Others

There are people around you who can teach you a lot. Jeter learned how to make double plays from another player on his team. Look around and find people who inspire you and teach you new things.

4. Give Back

Jeter's mom and dad taught him that it's important to help other people. He even started a foundation to help teenagers stay away from drugs and alcohol. Helping others can keep you grounded and focused on your journey.

5. Embrace Mistakes

To reach your goals, you have to take chances, and sometimes that means making mistakes. Jeter says it's okay to mess up. In fact, mistakes are important because they help you learn and grow.

6. Surround Yourself with Good People

Make friends with people who share your goals. They'll inspire you, encourage you, and cheer you on when things get tough.

7. Work Hard and Have Fun

Success takes a lot of hard work, but it's also important to do something you love and have fun with it. Jeter loved playing baseball, and he believes that's one of the reasons he did so well.

8. Think Before You Act

Jeter saw some players get distracted by the big city and forget about their game. He says it's important to think about your actions and not let anything distract you from your goals.

9. Be Ready

Jeter spent a lot of time learning about baseball and practicing his skills. Being ready for whatever comes your way is a big part of being successful.

10. Stay Humble

No matter how good you get, Jeter says it's important to stay humble. Remember where you came from, and always be kind to others.

The 4-C Model

Peter Clough, a smart brainy-guy, thought of a cool way to understand how tough our mind can be. He called it the 4C model. It's like the secret recipe for being mentally tough in sports! Let's see what each 'C' stands for:

Challenge: Think of challenges as secret adventures or quests. The more quests you complete, the stronger and wiser you become! It's like playing a video game where every level makes you better.

Control: Imagine you're the captain of your ship. You're the one who decides where it goes and what it does. Even when big waves come, you believe you can sail through!

Commitment: Imagine you're on a treasure hunt. No matter how hard it gets, you don't give up because you know there's a shiny treasure waiting for you at the end!

Confidence: Believe in yourself, just like a superhero does! Even when things get tough, a superhero never stops believing in their superpowers.

And then there's Angela Duckworth. She's another brainy person who thinks mental toughness is all about "grit". Grit is like being a brave knight who keeps going, even when the dragon is really big and scary. She even found out that the toughest and most successful knights aren't always the smartest, but they're the grittiest!

She thinks we can all be gritty knights in three steps:

Step 1: Decide what grit means to you. Maybe it's practicing your soccer kicks every day for a month without missing one.

Step 2: Become grittier by winning little victories. It's like doing one more math problem, running one more lap, or reading one more page every day. These small wins are like power-ups that make your grit grow!

Step 3: Make good habits your superpowers. Just like brushing your teeth every day, doing little things regularly can help you become grittier. You don't have to wait for a lightning bolt of bravery, just do your best every day!

Now, you might wonder, "what is mental toughness anyway?" Well, it's like a superhero power! It helps you believe in yourself, calms your worries, and lifts you over tricky situations that might stop you from reaching your dreams. Whether you're a star athlete, a boss, or someone just like you who wants to do their best, mental toughness can be your secret weapon!

You might be born with a bit of this superhero power, but even if you aren't, don't worry! You can still learn to be more determined, focused, brave, and in control when things get tough.

Let me tell you why mental toughness is like a superhero power. Imagine you're a superhero named Drew Shamrock. You say, "Without a strong mind, you can't be a real superhero. Have you ever skipped a workout or missed a football practice because you felt tired? It's usually your mind, not your body, telling you that. So, a superhero needs a strong mind to do their best!"

By building your mental superhero power, you can live the best life ever.

Here are five awesome things you'll notice:

1. Enjoy Life More:

As you grow your mental strength, you'll learn to like yourself more and always aim for better. This will help you enjoy life, even when it's a bit tough.

2. Be Your Best:

Whatever you dream of doing, mental strength helps you do it the best way you can. You can focus on what's important by controlling your thoughts, calming your feelings, and acting in a helpful way.

3. Be Strong in Tough Times:

Life can be like a tricky puzzle, but mental strength helps you solve it. You'll learn to deal with any problem that comes your way.

4. *Think Like a Winner:*

Your mind is like a big filter. If you think negative thoughts, you might not do so well. But if you have a winning mindset, you can do amazing things!

5. *Be Brave and Strong:*

Being a leader isn't just about winning. True leaders know that tough times are a part of the journey. They face problems bravely and push themselves to get over hurdles. They see difficulties as chances to grow and become stronger and braver.

Now that you know what mental toughness is and why it's super cool, you're ready to start your journey to become mentally stronger! Let's go, superhero!

Imagine you're in the final year of school and you're playing baseball against one of the best teams around. You're up against the first batter, who is really good. You try to throw a tricky ball, hoping he'll miss, but he doesn't. This happens again and again. It feels like it lasts forever, but these moments are the ones that make playing baseball so exciting. Even though it's hard, that's what makes it fun.

Sometimes, people only care about winning or doing well. We're told to focus on hitting a home run, losing weight, doing well in school, or other achievements, but what about the effort we put in? What about the hard times before the win?

For someone who likes to exercise, the real reward is not just losing weight or getting stronger, but challenging their body. For a writer, the real reward is not just having a best-selling book, but the joy of writing. For a sports player, the real reward is not just winning the game, but the fun of playing.

The effort to do something meaningful is the real reward. The chance to work hard and create something valuable. It's not just about the end result, but the little steps and challenges along the way. The effort itself is the prize. So don't ignore these tough moments, appreciate them! They're what makes life truly exciting.

Now, it might be hard to like an activity you really don't enjoy. But if there's a task you don't like but know is good for you, like exercising, there are two ways you can learn to like it.

First, you can get better at it. Even things you're good at can be boring sometimes, so imagine how hard it is to keep doing something you're not good at yet. To make this easier, learn the basics of the task and celebrate little victories. For example, if you don't like going to the gym, get a book about exercises and learn the right way to do them. As you get better, you might start to enjoy it.

Second, you can focus on what you get from the task instead of the task itself. For example, running really fast can always be tough. But what if you make it a game to never miss a workout day? By thinking about the goal instead of the task, you might find it easier to handle the boring parts.

Remember, the key to success is being patient and sticking with it. Doing the basics that everyone knows but often find too boring to do consistently can help you succeed. So, instead of trying to come up with new things, just keep doing what works, like practicing catching and hitting the ball. Even though it's hard, being consistent and dedicated can help you succeed.

The ROOKIE

Have you ever heard about Jim Morris? His story is like something from a movie - and in fact, they did make a movie about his life!

Jim was a 35-year-old high school baseball coach who made a special promise to his team. He told them if they won the district championship, he would try out for the big leagues, meaning the best baseball teams. And guess what? In 1999, his team won the championship! So, Jim kept his promise and went to try out for the big leagues.

At first, the people from the Tampa Bay Devil Rays team didn't really want to let Jim try out, but they did because he had made that promise to his students. Everyone was shocked when they found out that Jim could throw a ball really, really fast - 98 miles per hour! That's faster than a cheetah can run! Because he did so well, he got to play for the Durham Bulls, one of the Rays' teams.

And then something even more amazing happened.
The Tampa Bay Devil Rays let Jim play for their top team,
and on September 18, 1999, he got his first chance to pitch.
He did an amazing job and struck out another player on
just four throws.

Jim's story shows us that if you really, really want something, don't give up, no matter what! Even when things are
hard, or when it feels like you're too old, or when people
say you can't do it. Just imagine how brave Jim must have
been to play baseball with people half his age. His story
teaches us that when you refuse to be beaten and give your
best, amazing things can happen.

Conclusion

Becoming a mentally strong athlete is a lot like being a
super hero. Super heroes always do their best, no matter
what's happening. They're brave, focused, and don't let
anything stop them. That's what we call "mental toughness," and you can learn it too!

Think about when you're playing a game or a sport. Are
there times when you do really well? And are there times

when you don't do so well? It's important to think about how you feel in both situations. When you're doing well, you might feel really confident, like you're in control and nothing can stop you. That's what being mentally tough feels like!

But what about when you make a mistake, or when things are hard? Do you stay calm and keep trying, or do you feel frustrated and upset? If you feel upset, that's okay - everyone feels that way sometimes. But a super hero - or a mentally tough athlete - knows how to stay calm and keep trying, even when things are hard.

So if you want to be a mentally tough athlete, start by thinking about how you feel when you're playing. Practice feeling confident, staying focused, and staying calm, even when things are tough. Just like a super hero, you'll learn how to do your best, no matter what!

Chapter 2
The Importance
of Commitment

On a bright and sunny afternoon, the field buzzed with activity. The Mighty Cubs were gathered for practice, and the two newbies, Timmy and Bobby, were feeling a mix of excitement and jitters.

Coach Allen called, "Alright, Cubs, line up!" His voice echoed across the field, as the boys scampered to their positions, their shoes kicking up dust clouds.

The first challenge was handling grounders. The coach smacked the ball towards Timmy. It zipped across the green, like a streak of light. "Thunk!" It hit Timmy's glove but slipped right out, dancing away on the grass. Timmy's heart sank a little.

Bobby, watching Timmy, took a deep breath. Then, he saw the ball rocketing towards him. But, "Zoom!" it darted right between his legs and sprinted away into the outfield. Bobby's cheeks flushed with disappointment.

Next came the fly balls. Coach Allen launched a high one to Timmy. He kept his eyes on it as it sailed into the clear blue sky. But "Whoosh," it slipped past his out-stretched glove and landed with a soft plop behind him. Timmy clenched his fists, feeling a twinge of frustration.

Bobby reached out for his fly ball, but "Thud," it bounced off his glove and onto the grass with a sound that seemed louder in the silence of his disappointment.

The boys exchanged a look, their faces red with the e-ffort and their hearts heavy with frustration. They felt as though they had let their team down. The field, usually echoing with the sounds of joy and teamwork, seemed to be wrapped in a shroud of their frustration.

However, seeing their determined faces, Coach Allen rallied the team. "Listen up, Cubs," he said, "I know today is hard. You're going to make mistakes, and that's perfectly okay. That's how we learn. Remember, the key is to stay committed to getting better, to succeeding. That's what being a Mighty Cub is all about!"

Timmy and Bobby looked at each other, their resolve solidifying. They knew that they were facing a challenge, but they also knew they were committed to overcoming it. They would not quit. They were Mighty Cubs, after all!

The practice continued, and while the boys made a few more mistakes, they tackled each one with renewed resolve. They weren't just learning to play baseball; they were learning about the power of commitment to overcome life's hurdles. And they were committed to the journey!

What is Commitment?

Imagine this - you want to play with your favorite toy, but it's on the highest shelf. You're interested in playing with it, but will you make the effort to climb and reach it? That's the difference between being interested and being committed. When you're committed to something, you're like a super-kid who doesn't let anything stop them.

Once, there was a team of young baseball players who were getting ready for a big game. Their coach, named Mike, didn't shout or give a loud pep talk. Instead, he told them a story about a dad who loved his daughter so much that he would do anything to make her well again, even when it was really hard.

The dad was heavy and needed to lose weight so he could give his daughter a kidney she needed to get better. The dad didn't let anything stop him. He lost over 100 pounds in 6 months because he loved his daughter more than anything.

Mike compared the dad's strong commitment to what the baseball players needed to win their game. They needed to be strong, work hard, and never give up, just like the dad.

Then, Coach Mike talked about a baseball player named Shohei Ohtani. Even though Shohei is one of the best players in the world, he always wants to get better. Once, after winning a big game, Shohei didn't go to a party or take a break. He went to practice even more!

Shohei is a great example of someone who keeps their promise and works hard, even when nobody is watching.

So, let's think about your own promise. Do you promise to reach for your goals, like reaching for that toy on the highest shelf? Do you promise to work hard, just like Shohei and the dad in the story? Remember, it takes more than wanting something to get it - you need to make a strong promise and never give up!

So it's time to ask yourself, How serious are you about getting better at sports? There's a cool thing we can use to measure how much you're really into it. It's called the "Commitment Continuum." It's like a measuring stick for how much you want to improve and help your team.

So what's the Commitment Continuum? A man named Jeff Janson talked about it in his book. He says it's like a ladder with 6 steps. Here's what each step looks like:

1. RESISTANT: These players are a bit stubborn. They don't really want to work together for the team's goal. They're like horses pulling in different directions!

2. RELUCTANT: These players are unsure. They don't put in their full effort and excitement because they're not sure if their hard work will pay off. But with some encouragement and patience from their coaches and friends, they can become part of the team and do well.

3. EXISTENT: These players are physically there in the team but not really with their mind and heart. They're like sleepwalkers! They too need a bit of time and encouragement to really become part of the team.

4. COMPLIANT: These players do what they're told but don't try to do more than that. They understand the game and do what the coach says, but they need a lot of direction and motivation.

5. COMMITTED: These players are the real team players! They set their own goals and work hard to achieve them. They don't need someone to constantly push them. They're usually very successful.

6. COMPELLED: These are the superstars of the team! They're always positive and look for ways to get better.

They listen to their coaches and keep trying to play at the top level.

Now, think about it. Where are you on this ladder? Are you just going through the moves at practice? Or are you giving it your all?

The Commitment Continuum is like a secret tool. By knowing where you are on it, you can work to climb higher and help your team to win more games!

Okay, we've chatted about mind power. But our bodies are important too! Just like we exercise our minds, we have to exercise our bodies. Let's talk about some ways to get physically stronger for baseball.

First up is SPEED! Do you want to run faster? To boost your speed, try exercises like jump squats, bounding drills, and depth jumps. These will make your legs stronger and help you take bigger steps when you run. Plus, getting faster also helps make your muscles stronger, burn off energy, and keep you safe from injuries.

Next, let's talk about AGILITY. Agility is about moving smoothly and quickly. Agility exercises can help you move better and not get hurt. They also make you better at catching and hitting a ball, and they help your brain, balance, and coordination. It's like being a gymnast on the baseball field!

Now, let's discuss FLEXIBILITY. To play baseball, you need to be able to move easily. Flexibility is about more than touching your toes; it's about your body being able to move in all kinds of ways. If you're more flexible, your muscles and joints will be healthier, and you'll move better on the baseball field.

But there are two types of stretches, STATIC and DYNAMIC. Static stretching is when you stretch and hold it for a bit. It's not a good idea to do this before a game because it might make you slower. It's better to do this after the game or to relax your muscles.

Dynamic stretching is moving your joints and muscles in big ways. This is a good warm-up before a game and helps your body be ready to run, jump, and swing. You can do things like leg swings, walking lunges, hip circles, and arm circles. This helps your muscles warm up, makes you more flexible, and helps you play better in the game.

Remember, to be a great baseball player, you need to commit to getting stronger both in your mind and your body!

Okay, let's talk about EXPLOSIONS! Not the kind that go BOOM, but the kind that happens in your body when you need to be super fast or super strong, like when you're running really fast, hitting a baseball, or jumping high. To get really good at these, you need to exercise certain muscles.

Imagine these muscles are like little rockets inside your body, ready to blast you off into a sprint, jump, or throw. You can train these 'rocket muscles' by doing exercises like sprinting, throwing a medicine ball, and jumping. No more long, slow jogs! Instead, think of quick, powerful movements. This can help you run faster, hit harder, and jump higher!

Next, let's think about how much you TRAIN. You can't just exercise once a week and expect to become a superstar. You need to keep doing it, again and again. Think about it this way: who do you think would get better - a kid who practices with a fancy trainer for one hour a week or a kid who practices for an hour every day after school?

And, what about the QUALITY of your training? When you're practicing, you should be thinking about what you're doing. You shouldn't be daydreaming about what you're having for dinner. Remember, it's not just about how much weight you can lift or how many balls you can catch. It's about doing each rep and each exercise properly.

Finally, don't forget to have FUN! If you're enjoying what you're doing, it won't feel like work. Love your sport and be the first one at practice and the last one to leave.

But, what if you're not having fun anymore? What if playing baseball feels like a job? If that happens, it's okay. You might just be tired. Take a break, try new things, and do other stuff you love. Most importantly, be kind to yourself.

Remember, playing baseball is about having fun and doing your best. So keep practicing, stay focused, and keep enjoying the game!

Chapter 3
Overcoming Fear: Unleashing Your Inner Courage

D id you know that even the best athletes can feel nervous when they're competing? It's true! They might worry about making mistakes or letting their team down. But guess what? That pressure isn't real. It's all in their heads!

Let me tell you a story about Jason Kuhn, a Navy SEAL and a baseball player. He had to do a really tough swim in the ocean, and it scared him a lot. His trainers even made it scarier by showing videos of sharks and covering them in fish blood. But then something amazing happened.

Jason and his buddies came together and started saying a prayer. Suddenly, their fear disappeared, and they felt excited instead of scared. They realized that the pressure they felt was just in their minds. It wasn't real. And they knew they could handle anything that came their way.

Jason learned a valuable lesson from that experience. He realized that pressure is something we create ourselves. We worry too much about what others think and about being perfect. But the truth is, we should focus on enjoying the game and doing our best.

Jason has three tips to help us overcome fear and perform our best:

1. Play without pressure. Forget about the outcome and just focus on having fun and doing your best. Don't worry about what others think or about statistics. Enjoy the game!

2. Be thankful. Remember to be grateful for what you have. There's always someone who wishes they could be

in your shoes. Being grateful can help you have a positive mindset.

3. Boost your confidence. Before a game, talk to yourself and say positive things like "I can do this!" You can also listen to your favorite song that gets you pumped up. These things can help you feel confident and ready to do your best.

So remember, pressure isn't real. It's all about how you think about it. Stay positive, have fun, and give it your all. You'll be amazed at what you can achieve!

Fear can be ENERGIZING!

Did you know that feeling nervous or scared before a big game or competition is normal? It happens to the best athletes in the world! But did you also know that you can use that fear to your advantage? Let me tell you how.

When you feel a little bit nervous, it means that you care about what you're doing. Just like Rory McIlroy, a famous golfer, who gets nervous before playing in important tournaments. He sees it as a sign that he really wants to do well. That's a good thing!

But sometimes, stress can be too much. It can make you feel worried and anxious, and that's not good for your performance or your health. Your body also gets involved when you're stressed. It releases chemicals that make you feel on high alert, like something dangerous is happening.

So, how can you tell the difference between good stress and bad stress? It's all about finding the right balance. You want to feel excited and energized, but not so much that you can't think straight. You need to find that sweet spot where you're pumped up and focused at the same time.

And guess what? You have the power to turn that stress into excitement and motivation. When you feel those jitters before an important moment in the game, take a step back and reset your mind. Remind yourself that you can handle it and that you're ready for the challenge. Shift your perspective and believe in yourself.

You'll be amazed at how that simple change in thinking can make a big difference. It's like magic! So, embrace the nerves, use them to fuel your performance, and show everyone what you're capable of. You've got this!

Mighty Cubs

Timmy and Bobby had been friends since they were little. They grew up playing baseball together in their neighborhood, dreaming of one day becoming great players. But as much as they loved the game, Timmy always seemed to struggle more than Bobby.

Timmy's journey hadn't been easy. He had faced many challenges and setbacks along the way. He remembered a particular memory from when he was younger, playing in a Little League game. It was the championship game, and the pressure was high. Timmy had a chance to hit the winning run, but when he stepped up to the plate, fear took over. He swung and missed, and then swung and missed again. The disappointment on his face was evident as he struck out, ending the game.

That memory haunted Timmy for a long time. He started doubting his abilities and became fearful of failure. Every time he stepped onto the field, he carried the weight of that past failure with him.

But as the important game approached, Timmy knew that he couldn't let his fear hold him back anymore. He wanted to prove to himself and his team that he could overcome his challenges and succeed.

As the game began, Timmy found himself in the outfield, a position that had always made him nervous. The opposing team's best hitter came up to bat, and Timmy's heart started to race. Memories of past mistakes flooded his mind, and he could feel fear creeping in once again.

But then, in that moment of fear, Timmy's mind shifted. He remembered the support and encouragement from Bobby, his family, and his coach. He realized that failure was a part of the game, and it didn't define him as a person or a player. He decided to let go of the fear and focus on doing his best.

As the batter hit a powerful line drive towards him, Timmy's instincts kicked in. He sprinted towards the ball, feeling a surge of determination and confidence building within him. He could hear the cheers of his teammates, urging him on.

With perfect timing and a leap of faith, Timmy stretched his glove high into the air, reaching for the ball. The moment seemed to freeze as the ball landed securely in his glove. The crowd erupted into applause, and his teammates rushed over to celebrate the incredible catch.

Timmy couldn't help but smile. He had conquered his fear, and in that moment, he felt a sense of triumph like never before. He realized that his past failures didn't define him. They were stepping stones to growth and learning. He had finally let go of the fear that had held him back for so long, and it had paid off.

From that day forward, Timmy played with a newfound sense of confidence and determination. He still faced challenges and made mistakes, but he no longer let them consume him. He embraced the lessons learned from failure and used them as fuel to push himself further.

With each game, Timmy continued to improve, surprising himself and everyone around him. He became known for his incredible catches and clutch hits. But more importantly, he became an inspiration to others who were struggling with their own fears and doubts.

Timmy and Bobby continued their baseball journey together, supporting each other every step of the way. They celebrated their victories and learned from their failures, knowing that the most important thing was their commitment to never give up and to always believe in themselves.

And as they looked ahead to a future filled with more challenges and opportunities, they knew that no matter what came their way, they had the strength and determination to overcome it. They were a team united by their shared commitment to succeed, and their journey was just beginning.

Chapter 4
Nurturing Confidence: Building a Strong Foundation

Confidence is like a superpower that can make you soar in baseball and in life. When you believe in yourself, amazing things can happen! That's why building self-confidence is such an important skill for ballplayers.

Sometimes, you might feel unsure or worried. That's okay! Everyone goes through ups and downs. But the good news is, you can learn to boost your confidence and keep it strong. Just like practicing a sport, you can practice being confident too!

One way to build confidence is by setting goals for yourself. These goals should be challenging but also achievable. When you work hard and see yourself making progress, your confidence grows.

It's also helpful to have coaches and teammates who support you. They can encourage you, show you new skills, and cheer you on. When you see others believe in you, it boosts your own belief in yourself.

Remember, the way you talk to yourself matters too. Instead of saying negative things like "I can't do it," tell yourself positive things like "I can do this!" Be your own biggest cheerleader.

Even if things don't always go perfectly, it's important to keep believing in yourself. Your worth as a person doesn't depend on how well you play the game. Your family and friends will always care about you no matter what.

So, keep practicing, keep pushing yourself, and never let your confidence waver. Believe in yourself, and you'll achieve great things on and off the baseball field. You've got what it takes!

Are you ready to become even more confident in your athletic abilities? Here are seven important rules that will help you build unbreakable confidence. Get ready to soar to new heights!

Rule #1: Focus on yourself.

Instead of comparing yourself to others, focus on your own strengths and weaknesses. Set goals for yourself and work towards them. Remember, you are unique and have your own special talents!

Rule #2: Be kind to yourself.

Mistakes happen to everyone, and that's okay! Instead of being too hard on yourself, be constructive and learn from your mistakes. Celebrate your successes along the way and give yourself some love.

Rule #3: Embrace being a work in progress.

Nobody is perfect, and that includes athletes. Understand that you are always learning and growing. Don't worry about being perfect, focus on making progress and becoming better every day.

Rule #4: Practice makes progress.

The more you practice, the better you'll become. Make time every day to practice your skills, whether it's dribbling a basketball or kicking a soccer ball. With practice, you'll become more confident and skilled.

Rule #5: Emotions come and go.

Sometimes you'll feel excited and happy, and other times you might feel frustrated or disappointed. Remember that these emotions are temporary. Use them as motivation to work harder and bounce back stronger.

Rule #6: Believe in your potential.

Know that you have the ability to improve and grow through hard work and dedication. Believe in yourself and your potential. When you have a positive mindset, you'll be more resilient and ready to take on any challenge.

These rules will help you build unbreakable confidence as an athlete. Remember, you're amazing just the way you are, and with practice and a positive mindset, you'll achieve great things. Keep believing in yourself, and let your confidence shine bright!

Rule #7: Never stop chasing your athletic dreams.

When things get tough or you face challenges, it can be tempting to give up. But always remember why you started playing your sport in the first place. Keep that passion alive and let it be your fuel to keep going.

Whether you dream of becoming an Olympic athlete or just want to get better at your favorite game, never give up on your athletic dreams. Believe in yourself and your abilities. With hard work, dedication, and a positive attitude, you can achieve anything you set your mind to.

It's okay to have setbacks and face obstacles along the way. Don't let them discourage you. Use them as learning experiences and stepping stones to become even better. Keep pushing forward, keep practicing, and keep believing in yourself. Your dreams are within reach if you never give up!

So, my young athlete, remember to always chase your dreams with determination and perseverance. Believe in yourself, stay focused, and keep working hard. The road may have bumps, but with passion and a never-give-up attitude, you can make your athletic dreams come true.

The Power of Positive Thinking

Have you ever felt down and doubted yourself during a game? Maybe you missed a shot or made a mistake, and it made you feel like you're not good enough. But guess what? You have the power to change those negative thoughts and boost your confidence.

Your subconscious mind is like a superpower that can help you perform better. It's like a little voice inside your head that can either lift you up or bring you down. So let's train your subconscious mind to think positively and believe in yourself!

Exercise #1: Positive Pep Talk

Every day, take five minutes to think about the things you said to yourself. Were they positive or negative? If you caught yourself saying mean things like "I'm not good enough" or "I can't do it," stop right there! Replace those negative thoughts with positive ones. Tell yourself things like "I can do it" or "I am getting better every day." The more you say positive things to yourself, the stronger your subconscious mind will become.

Exercise #2: Picture Your Success

Close your eyes and imagine yourself playing your sport. See yourself hitting the ball perfectly, scoring goals, or making amazing passes. Picture yourself being confident and successful. Feel the excitement and joy of achieving your goals. This is called visualization, and it's a powerful tool that athletes use to improve their performance.

Let's take an example from Serena Williams, a famous tennis player. Before an important match, Serena would imagine herself hitting powerful shots and moving smoothly on the court. She would see herself winning the game and feel the happiness of victory. By doing this, she trained her mind to be ready for the match.

When the day of the championship arrived, Serena felt confident and focused. She played with skill and grace, just like she visualized. And guess what? She won the game and became the champion!

You can use visualization too! Before your game or practice, take a few moments to picture yourself succeeding. Imagine every detail, from your movements to your emotions. This will help your subconscious mind believe in your abilities and boost your confidence.

Remember, your mind is a powerful tool. By training your subconscious to think positively and visualize success, you can become a more confident athlete. So keep practicing these exercises, believe in yourself, and watch your performance soar!

The Story of Mike Piazza

Let me tell you an amazing story about a baseball player named Mike Piazza. His journey to the Baseball Hall of Fame is truly inspiring!

Back in 1988, during the MLB draft, Mike Piazza was picked by the Los Angeles Dodgers in the 62nd round. Now, that's a really late round, and most players picked that late don't usually make it to the big leagues. Many people thought Piazza was only picked as a "favor" because he was friends with the team manager, Tommy Lasorda.

But you know what? Instead of feeling discouraged, Piazza used that as motivation. He knew people doubted him, so he worked even harder to prove them wrong. And guess what? In 1992, he finally got his chance to play in the major leagues.

Once Piazza got his chance, he never looked back. He became one of the best catchers in the entire league! In 1993, he even won the National League Rookie of the Year award. His mighty swing and ability to hit for both average and power made him a force to be reckoned with.

Throughout his career, Piazza played for different teams like the Dodgers, the New York Mets, and the San Diego Padres. He was incredibly talented and accomplished so much. He was selected as an All-Star player seven times and won the prestigious Silver Slugger award ten times!

In 2016, Piazza's hard work and dedication paid off when he was inducted into the Baseball Hall of Fame. This means he's considered one of the greatest catchers in the history of the game! It's an incredible achievement that shows how anything is possible if you believe in yourself and never give up.

So remember, just like Mike Piazza, you can achieve greatness too. Work hard, stay determined, and always believe in yourself. Who knows? Maybe one day you'll make it to the Hall of Fame too!

Chapter 5
Embracing Sacrifice: The Pathway to Success

B obby loved playing baseball more than anything else in the world. He would eagerly look forward to every practice and game, ready to give his all on the field. But there was one day when Bobby really didn't want to sacrifice something for baseball, and it taught him an important lesson.

It was a warm summer afternoon, and the baseball team had an important practice scheduled. Bobby's family had planned a trip to the water park, something they had been looking forward to for a long time. When Bobby's mom told him about the trip, he felt torn. He didn't want to miss out on the fun with his family, but he also didn't want to miss the practice.

Bobby tried to convince himself that skipping one practice wouldn't make much of a difference. He thought he could make it up by practicing extra hard the next day. But deep down, he knew that missing a practice would mean letting his teammates down and not giving his best effort.

Reluctantly, Bobby decided to talk to his parents about his dilemma. He explained how much he loved baseball and how important the practice was for the team. His parents, understanding his passion, encouraged him to make the sacrifice and attend the practice. They assured him that they would plan another fun family outing soon.

As Bobby arrived at the practice, he felt a mix of emotions. He felt sad about missing the water park trip, but he also felt proud of himself for making the sacrifice for his team. However, there was still a part of him that felt a little disappointed.

During practice, Bobby watched his teammates working hard and supporting each other. He realized that he was part of something bigger than himself—a team that relied on each other's commitment and dedication. As he joined in the drills and participated in the practice, Bobby started feeling better. He knew he had made the right choice.

After practice, Bobby shared his feelings with his coach. He expressed how difficult it had been to make the sacrifice, but also how proud he felt for being there and giving his best. The coach smiled and commended Bobby for his commitment and understanding of the importance of sacrifices.

From that day forward, Bobby learned the importance of sacrifices in his baseball journey. He understood that sometimes, to achieve something meaningful, he would have to give up certain things. He realized that sacrifice was not just about missing out on one event, but about showing dedication, responsibility, and respect for his teammates and the sport he loved.

Bobby's experience taught him that sacrifices were not always easy, but they were a part of becoming a better player and teammate. He learned to embrace the value of sacrifice and to always think about the bigger picture—how his dedication and commitment would contribute to the success of the team. And as Bobby continued to grow as a baseball player, he carried that valuable lesson with him, knowing that sacrifices were an essential part of reaching his full potential on the field.

Making Sacrifices for Success

Sometimes, achieving success means making sacrifices along the way. When you want to become the best at something, you have to work hard and give up other things. Let's talk about some of the sacrifices that athletes make to reach the top.

Physical Sacrifices:

To be really good at a sport, athletes have to train a lot and push themselves to their limits. This means they might have to give up some comfort, like staying in bed or taking it easy. They have to take care of their bodies and understand that injuries and setbacks can happen. It's all part of the journey.

Relational Sacrifices:

Athletes often have to give up time with their friends and family to focus on their sport. They might miss parties or other fun events because they have practices or games. It's not always easy, but they know that their loved ones support them and understand their goals. Balancing sports and relationships is important.

Time Sacrifices:

Becoming really good at a sport takes a lot of time. Athletes have to spend hours practicing, training, and competing. This means they might have to wake up early or stay up late. They have to be willing to give up other activities to devote their time to their sport.

Monetary Sacrifices:

Sometimes, being a great athlete can be expensive. Athletes might have to spend money on equipment, training, and travel expenses. They might also have to say no to job opportunities that pay a lot of money because they want to focus on their sport. It can be a big sacrifice, but they know it's worth it.

Mental Sacrifices:

Athletes have to be mentally strong and focused on their goals. They have to stay positive even when things get tough. They might face setbacks or failures, but they keep going. It takes a lot of mental strength to keep working hard and never give up.

Injuries:

Playing sports can be risky, and sometimes athletes get injured. It can happen from overusing their bodies or accidents on the field. Injuries can be painful and take time to heal. They can even affect athletes after they retire from their sport. It's a risk that comes with playing sports, but athletes are willing to take that risk for their passion.

Remember, achieving success often means making sacrifices. It's not always easy, but if you're passionate about something and willing to work hard, the sacrifices will be worth it. Keep pushing forward and never give up on your dreams!

Hank Aaron's Amazing Journey

Let me tell you an incredible story about a baseball player named Hank Aaron. He had a dream of becoming a professional baseball player when he was just a young boy. He loved playing with his friends in the backyard, pretending to hit home runs and make amazing catches like a real superstar!

But growing up in Mobile, Alabama in the 1940s and 1950s wasn't easy for Hank. His family didn't have a lot of money, and racism was very common in the Deep South. Despite these tough challenges, Hank was determined to make his dream come true.

As a teenager, Hank had to work after school and on weekends to help his family. But he never gave up on his dream. Every spare moment he had, he would practice his swing, catch grounders, and run drills. Sometimes, he even had to make his own baseball equipment out of scrap materials because he couldn't afford to buy them.

When Hank turned 18, he joined the Negro Leagues and played for a team called the Indianapolis Clowns. He had to leave his family and friends behind and travel all around the country to play in games. It was really tough because he had to face harsh living conditions and didn't earn much money. And in some cities, he had to deal with segregation, where people were treated unfairly based on the color of their skin. But Hank never gave up. He kept working hard and getting better at the game.

Then, in 1954, Hank's dream came true! He was signed by the Milwaukee Braves and became a Major League Baseball player. Even though he made it to the big leagues, Hank still faced racism and discrimination. He received scary death threats and hateful letters. But he didn't let that stop him. He kept going and didn't give up on his dream.

For the next 23 years, Hank Aaron became one of the greatest baseball players in history. He hit an incredible 755 home runs and won lots of awards and honors. His story inspired many people and helped make a better future for athletes of all backgrounds.

Hank Aaron's journey shows us that we should never give up on our dreams, no matter how challenging things may be. He worked hard, faced tough times, and never stopped believing in himself. So remember, if you have a dream, keep working towards it with all your heart. Who knows? Maybe one day you'll achieve something amazing, just like Hank Aaron!

As a student-athlete, it can be challenging to balance school and sports. But don't worry, there are ways to manage it! Here are some tips:

1. Stay focused: When you're doing schoolwork, focus only on that. When you're playing sports, focus on that too. Don't mix the two.

2. Prioritize: Figure out which tasks are most important and do them first. Take it one step at a time.

3. Plan ahead: Make a schedule for your days and weeks. Know when you'll study and when you'll practice.

4. Avoid distractions: Put your phone away and stay away from things that can distract you. Say no to friends if you need to focus.

5. Ask for help: If you have a lot of work, ask your teachers for more time. They might give you an extension.

6. Don't skip practice: Even if you have lots of schoolwork, it's important to go to practice. Exercise helps reduce stress.

7. Make healthy choices: Eat a balanced diet and drink plenty of water. Get enough sleep too, at least 7 hours a night.

Remember, finding balance is important. By following these tips and making sacrifices, you can achieve your athletic dreams while still doing well in school. You can do it!

Chapter 6
Setting Goals: Mapping Your Journey to Greatness

Goal setting is super important in sports! It helps athletes perform their best. Setting goals means deciding what you want to achieve and how you'll get there. But it's not just about any goal - it's about setting goals that focus on the process and how you perform, not just winning or losing.

Setting goals is important because it boosts motivation. When you have a specific goal, it gives you a clear direction and purpose in your training. It's like having a map to guide you!

Goal setting also boosts self-confidence. When you work hard and achieve a goal, you feel proud of yourself. It's like scoring a winning goal! It makes you believe in yourself and feel good about what you can do.

There are different types of goals, like short-term goals and long-term goals. Short-term goals are things you want to achieve soon, and long-term goals are your big dreams. It's important to set realistic goals that challenge you but are possible to achieve.

To achieve your goals, you need to work hard and never give up. Take small steps every day to get closer to your goals. Celebrate your progress along the way, even the small wins.

So, set goals that focus on improving yourself, stay motivated, and work hard. You've got what it takes to reach your goals!

Mighty Cubs

Timmy stood on the baseball field, gripping his bat tightly in his hands. He watched as the coach hit the ball, and he swung with all his might, but the ball flew past him. It was a swing and a miss. Timmy's heart sank. He felt frustrated and disappointed in himself. He wondered if he would ever get better at baseball.

As Timmy walked back to the dugout, Coach Johnson called him over. "Timmy, I noticed that you're having a tough time connecting with the ball. I want to talk to you about setting goals," Coach Johnson said.

Timmy looked at Coach Johnson with a puzzled expression. "What do you mean, Coach? How can goals help me hit the ball better?"

Coach Johnson smiled and replied, "Goals give you something to work towards and help you measure your progress. They help you focus on specific areas where you want to improve. Let's set a goal for you to make more solid contact with the ball during practice."

Timmy nodded, feeling a glimmer of hope. He realized that setting goals could help him become a better player. Coach Johnson continued, "Let's break down this goal into smaller steps. First, we'll work on your stance and swing technique. Then we'll practice your timing and hand-eye coordination."

Timmy's mind started buzzing with excitement. He imagined himself hitting the ball with precision, just like the big-league players on TV. He could almost hear the crack of the bat and feel the satisfaction of making solid contact.

The next practice, Timmy focused on his goal. He adjusted his stance, listened to the sound of the ball leaving the coach's hand, and swung with purpose. At first, he missed a few balls, but he didn't give up. He listened to Coach Johnson's encouraging words and tried again.

With each swing, Timmy could feel himself improving. He started making better contact with the ball, and it soared through the air. He could hear the satisfying thud as the ball hit the glove of the outfielder.

The more Timmy practiced, the more confident he became. He set new goals for himself, like hitting the ball to different parts of the field and improving his running speed. He could feel his skills improving, and he was excited to see what he could achieve.

One day, during a game, Timmy stepped up to the plate. He took a deep breath, remembered the goals he had set, and focused on making solid contact. As the pitcher wound up, Timmy swung his bat with precision and heard the sweet sound of the ball connecting with it. The ball soared into the outfield, far beyond the reach of the fielders.

Timmy's heart swelled with pride. He realized that setting goals and working hard to achieve them had paid off. He had come a long way from that swing and a miss he had experienced before. Timmy knew that with determination and the guidance of his coaches, he could continue to set goals and improve his skills.

From that day forward, Timmy embraced the power of setting goals in his baseball practices. He understood that they were the key to unlocking his potential and achieving success on the field. With each goal he set and surpassed, Timmy grew into a more confident and skilled player, ready to take on any challenge that came his way.

In the world of baseball, setting goals is like having a secret weapon that can make you a better player. It's like having a map that shows you the way to success. When you set goals, you give yourself a clear target to aim for and a plan to follow. Let's discover why setting goals is so important in baseball!

First of all, goals help you stay focused. Imagine you're a pitcher, and you want to improve your accuracy. By setting a goal to throw strikes more consistently, you'll pay extra attention to your form and practice that perfect pitch. With each practice, you'll see yourself getting closer to hitting the target, and it will make you more determined to keep trying.

Setting goals also helps you measure your progress. Think of it like a scoreboard in a game. When you set a goal to hit more home runs, you can keep track of how many you've hit and see if you're getting closer to your target. It's like a friendly competition with yourself!

Goals also give you motivation. When you have a specific goal in mind, like stealing more bases, you'll feel excited and driven to work hard. You'll imagine the thrill of sliding safely into the next base, and it will push you to improve your speed and technique.

Another important thing about goals is that they help you improve. Let's say you want to become a better fielder. By setting a goal to catch more fly balls during practice, you'll challenge yourself to be quicker and more focused. As you keep practicing, you'll notice your skills getting sharper, and soon you'll be making those incredible catches that amaze everyone!

Remember, goals aren't just about the final result. They're about the journey too. Along the way, you'll learn important lessons, like patience, perseverance, and teamwork. Sometimes you might face setbacks, but goals will keep you motivated to keep pushing forward.

So, my young baseball player, whether you want to improve your batting average, make better throws, or become an all-around player, start setting goals! Think about what you want to achieve and break it down into smaller steps. Practice hard, listen to your coaches, and believe in yourself. You'll be amazed at what you can accomplish when you have a goal to guide you. Get ready to hit those home runs and make incredible plays on the field!

Chapter 7
Resilience: Rising Strong After a Fall

C al Ripken Jr. is a famous baseball player who holds an incredible record of playing 2,632 consecutive games in Major League Baseball. But did you know that Ripken faced failures in his career too? Even though he was an All-Star player, he struggled with hitting early on.

Instead of giving up, Ripken saw his failures as chances to learn and get better. He asked for advice from coaches and teammates and studied his own performance. He worked hard to improve his swing and understand the pitchers he faced.

All his effort paid off! Ripken had a fantastic year in 1983, hitting .318 with many home runs. He kept getting better and finished his career with a .276 batting average.

But it wasn't just about his physical skills. Ripken had a positive mindset. He believed that every game was an opportunity to learn and grow. He said that failure is normal in baseball and that it's important to know how to deal with it. He never gave up and always stayed curious and open to learning.

We can learn from Ripken's approach. When we face failures or setbacks, we shouldn't give up. Instead, we should see them as chances to learn and improve. We can ask for feedback, practice hard, stay positive, and enjoy the journey. Like Ripken, we can turn failure into success!

Remember, failure doesn't have to stop you. With the right mindset and determination, you can overcome any challenge and achieve your goals. Keep trying, keep learning, and never give up!

Failure is something that happens to all of us, and it can actually teach us important lessons. When we try something and it doesn't work out, we learn what does and doesn't work. This is helpful because it shows us how to improve and try new strategies.

Sometimes, failure can also show us what's really important in life. It helps us understand what we truly care about and what goals we want to achieve.

When we fail, we can learn from others who have gone through similar experiences. By sharing our own stories of failure and how we overcame them, we can inspire and help others too.

Failure can also make us more creative. When things don't go as planned, we have to think of new ways to solve problems and find different approaches.

But most importantly, failure teaches us about ourselves. We learn about our strengths, weaknesses, and how to grow and become better. It's all part of the journey of becoming the best version of ourselves.

Remember, failure is not the end of the world. It's just a chance to learn and try again. Don't be afraid of it, but instead, embrace it as a teacher and use it to become even more successful in the future.

Here are some important lessons we can learn from failure:

1. Trying is brave and admirable.

2. Failure doesn't define you or your future.

3. Learn from your mistakes and take responsibility.

4. Failure helps you figure out what works and what doesn't.

5. Even successful people have failed many times.

6. Failure can show you how strong and resilient you are.

7. Mistakes are opportunities to learn and grow.

8. Keep trying and never give up.

9. Success and failure are both part of life's journey.

10. Learn from failure and use it to become even better.

Chapter 8
Mighty Cubs
Final Story

T immy and Bobby stood together, looking back on their amazing journey. They had come a long way since their first day playing baseball. The sun was setting, painting the field in beautiful golden colors, like it was celebrating their progress.

As they remembered the challenges they faced, they realized how their mental toughness had helped them overcome tough practices, mistakes, and moments of doubt. It wasn't always easy, but they discovered the power inside them that made them strong.

They learned important lessons from their baseball experiences that went beyond the game. They understood the value of working hard and never giving up on their goals. They discovered that with determination and never quitting, they could achieve anything they set their minds to.

But it wasn't just about winning games or hitting home runs. They discovered the true meaning of teamwork, supporting their teammates through good times and bad. They learned how to be good sports, celebrating not only their own victories but also those of their teammates and even their opponents.

Baseball became more than just a game for Timmy and Bobby. It became their teacher, helping them grow as people and teaching them lessons for life. They learned that setbacks and failures were not the end, but opportunities to become better. They faced challenges with bravery and always came back stronger.

Looking ahead, they knew their journey was not over. There would be more ups and downs, more challenges to overcome. But they were ready for anything. They had mental toughness, a love for the game, and the support of their teammates and coaches.

They became ambassadors of mental toughness, sharing their knowledge with others. They encouraged their friends to believe in themselves and never give up. They knew that mental toughness was not just for baseball, but for every part of life.

Timmy and Bobby realized that the most important thing was not the number of wins or trophies. It was the friendships they made, the memories they created, and the lessons they learned along the way.

As the sun went down, casting long shadows on the field, Timmy and Bobby knew their journey had only just begun. They were ready to face the future, hand in hand. With confidence in their hearts and determination in their minds, they were ready to make a difference, both in baseball and in the world.

Conclusion

You now know how important it is to train your mind to be strong as you chase your athletic dreams. In this book, we've talked about different ways to help young athletes like you, such as having a positive attitude, setting goals, imagining success, and bouncing back from challenges. By using these strategies, you can go onto the field every day feeling confident and ready to give it your all.

To all the young athletes out there, it's time to take charge of your sports journey! You have the ability to make your dreams come true, but it will take hard work and commitment. The techniques we've learned in this book about mental toughness will help you reach your goals and overcome any obstacles that come your way.

So don't wait. Start using the tips from this book today. Set your goals, imagine yourself doing great, and be
strong when things get tough. With these tools, you can
overcome challenges and do your best, both in sports and
in life.

Remember, mental toughness is not only for sports; it's
a skill that will help you in many areas of your life. So
take action, embrace the ideas of mental toughness, and
go after your dreams with excitement and determination.
You can do it!

Thank you for Reading!

Thank you for reading this book! If you enjoyed it or have any feedback, I would greatly appreciate it if you could take a moment to leave a review on Amazon. Your thoughts not only help improve the book but also support me as an author. You can leave a review by following this link: PLAY BALL REVIEW or by simply scanning the QR code provided. Thank you for your support and happy reading!

Baseball's All-Time Most Inspirational Quotes

*B*elow are some of the greatest quotes about baseball ever spoken. (Parents and coaches, share these with your children and reminisce about the first time you heard the quote and how it impacted you). Whether in movie or in real life, let these quotes inspire and fuel you to be the best player you can be! Read one each day and use it as a focus for your day. Eventually, you will be a well-rounded athlete that can handle anything that comes your way!

Enjoy!

"How can you not be romantic about baseball?"
—Moneyball

"You wanna have a catch?" —Field of Dreams

"Man, this is baseball. You gotta stop thinking, just have fun." —The Sandlot

"All I know is when we win a game, it's a team win. When we lose a game, it's a team loss." —The Bad News Bears

"There's no crying in baseball!" —A League of Their Own

"I see great things in baseball. It's our game, the American game. It will repair our losses and be a blessing to us all." —Bull Durham

"Baseball is dull only to dull minds." – Sportscaster, Red Barber

"Hello again, everybody. It's a bee-yoo-tiful day for baseball." – Sportscaster, Harry Caray

"Baseball has long been a national pastime that many Americans have cherished." – American Politician, Jim Sensenbrenner.

"The other sports are just sports. Baseball is a love." – Sportscaster, Bryant Gumbel

"Baseball, it is said, is only a game. True. And the Grand Canyon is only a hole in Arizona." – Journalist & Author, George Will

"A hot dog at the game beats roast beef at the Ritz." – American Actor, Humphrey Bogart

"Poets are like baseball pitchers. Both have their moments. The intervals are the tough things." – *American Poet, Robert Lee Frost*

"It could be, it might be...It is, a home run!" – *Sportscaster, Harry Caray*

"Baseball is more than a game to me, it's a religion." – *MLB Umpire, William 'Bill' Klem*

"It ain't nothin' till I call it." – *MLB Umpire, William 'Bill' Klem*

"As a kid, before I could play music, I remember baseball being the one thing that could always make me happy." Country Singer, Garth Brooks

"Baseball is more than a game. It's like life played out on a field." – Musician, Juliana Hatfield

"Progress always involves risk. You can't steal second base and keep your foot on first." – Frederick B. Wilcox

"Baseball is one of the most beautiful games. It is a very zen-like game." – American Film Director, Jim Jarmusch

"There are only two seasons: winter and baseball."
— Bill Veeck, Jr.

"Baseball is a lot like life. It's a day-to-day exis-
tence, full of ups and downs. You make the most of
your opportunities in baseball as you do in life." —
American Sportscaster, Ernie Harwell

"There are three types of baseball players: those
who make it happen, those who watch it happen,
and those who wonder what happened." — Tommy
Lasorda

"Baseball is like driving, it's the one who gets home
safely that counts." — Tommy Lasorda

"Bad ballplayers make great managers, not the other way around. All I can do is help them be as good as they are." – Earl Weaver

"A baseball manager is a necessary evil." – George 'Sparky' Anderson

"I've come to the conclusion that the two most important things in life are good friends and a good bullpen." – Bob Lemon

"The greatest feeling in the world is to win a major league game. The second greatest feeling is to lose a major league game." – Chuck Tanner

"I really love the togetherness in baseball. That's real true love." – Billy Martin

"Baseball is like church. Many attend, but few understand." – Leo Ernest Durocher

"Close doesn't count in baseball. Close only counts in horseshoes and grenades." – Frank Robinson

"Never save a pitcher for tomorrow. Tomorrow it may rain." – Leo Durocher

"Every strike brings me closer to the next home run." – Babe Ruth

"Every day is a new opportunity. You can build on yesterday's success or put its failures behind and start over again. That's the way life is, with a new game every day, and that's the way baseball is." – **Bullet Bob Feller**

"People ask me what I do in the winter when there's no baseball. I'll tell you what I do. I stare out the window and wait for spring." – **Rogers Hornsby**

"Playing baseball for a living is like having a license to steal." – **Pete Rose**

"Baseball is the only field of endeavor where a man can succeed three times out of ten and be considered a good performer." – **Ted Williams**

"When you start the game, they don't say "Work ball!" They say, "Play ball!"" – Willie Stargell. "

"The game had done much for me, and I had done much for it." – Jackie Robinson.

"Well, it took me 17 years to get 3,000 hits in baseball, and I did it in one afternoon on the golf course." – Hank Aaron

"If my uniform doesn't get dirty, I haven't done anything in the baseball game." – Rickey Henderson

Made in the USA
Monee, IL
28 October 2024

68731785R00056